ALONE WITH THE SAVIOR

Alone *with the* Savior

31 DAILY MEDITATIONS *on* CHRIST'S FAITHFULNESS

BILLY GRAHAM

Compiled from Decision magazine

BILLY GRAHAM EVANGELISTIC ASSOCIATION

Charlotte, North Carolina

Table *of* Contents

Alone with the Savior

ISBN: 978-1-59328-281-3

Foreword

My father has always loved to preach and write about Christ's faithfulness. I believe this is because he himself has experienced that sustaining faithfulness so deeply and personally in his own life over many years. For this hope-filled devotional book, we've selected 31 favorite excerpts from articles he authored over the years in *Decision* magazine. Each one is a brief meditation on some aspect of the faithfulness of Jesus Christ.

I pray that as you read and carefully consider these daily insights, you yourself will understand Jesus Christ more fully and experience His faithfulness more deeply than ever before.

We would appreciate hearing if you find this book helpful in your walk with Christ or if you have been touched by the ministry of the Billy Graham Evangelistic Association in other ways. To contact us, or to learn more about our ministry, see the information on the last page. May God richly bless you.

Franklin Graham
November 2010

Jesus Christ is the same yesterday and today and forever.
—HEBREWS 13:8

The Rainbow *of* Hope

Let me put a rainbow of hope in your heart. It has been proved millions of times over that Jesus Christ can meet and solve the basic problems of your life. This is the promise of Hebrews 13:8.

The word *yesterday* in that verse means the past—when He was on earth.

The word *today* means now, the present—when He is in Heaven. And the word *forever* looks into the future—when He shall return to earth to rule and reign.

Yesterday, the past, when He was on earth—He made atonement; He forgave and covered your sin, your past. Today, now, in Heaven—He is an advocate, representing before God those who place their trust in Him. He is right now willing to solve your problems, lift your burdens, wipe the tears away, and bring joy, peace, and satisfaction such as you have never known.

Tomorrow, in the future—He will return to be King of kings and Lord of lords.

Other things may change, but Christ will never change. We are living in an age of grace in which God promises that whosoever will may come and receive His Son.

When this age of grace ends, the judgment of God will strike and the world will suffer from the judgment hand of God.

But today I can offer you an unchanging Christ who can forgive your past sin, lift your present burdens, and give you hope for the future. He will take your sins and bury them in the depth of the sea.

Prayer *for the* Day:

Thank You, Lord Jesus, for providing forgiveness for my past, respite from today's burdens, and hope for all of my tomorrows. Help me to share Your hope with those around me.

The day of the Lord will come as a thief in the night.
—2 PETER 3:10, NKJV

_____

A Warning *and a* Promise

The flood was the greatest catastrophe in the history of the world. Scripture says that the flood destroyed everything. The importance of Noah and the flood is emphasized by the many references to it in the Bible.

The flood was both a warning and a promise. God warned that He would not always strive with man. Then He made a covenant with Noah and his sons that He would never again destroy the world by flood, and He gave the rainbow as a promise.

The Apostle Peter wrote that in Noah's day *"the world that then existed perished, being flooded with water"* (2 Peter 3:6, NKJV). But he also wrote that *"the day of the Lord will come as a thief in the night, in which the heavens will pass away with a great noise, and the elements will melt with fervent heat; both*

the earth and the works that are in it will be burned up"
(2 Peter 3:10, NKJV).

We do not know at what hour the Lord is coming back again. But we are told in Scripture that there will be signs pointing toward the return of the Lord. I believe that we see those signs in the world today. I believe that the coming of the Lord is near.

People today are concerned and frightened as they look at world conditions. Many things seem to be pointing toward that time.

The flood was not a natural catastrophe. The flood was a moral catastrophe. It came as a result of God's judgment on the attitudes and actions of the people in the world of that time. God has set a time limit for our day as well. God has *set a day when he will judge the world with justice by the man he has appointed* [*Christ Jesus*]*"* (Acts 17:31). We don't know when it is, but Jesus said the hour is coming.

Prayer *for the* Day:

Father, thank You for Your promise that Christ will return. Remind me daily that the hour of judgment is coming, so that I live in preparation for that day.

4

I am going ... to prepare a place for you. And if I go and prepare a place for you, I will come back and take you to be with me that you also may be where I am. —JOHN 14:2–3

A Place Prepared

God told Noah to build an ark, or ship, out in the desert. Noah had no place to sail the ship, but he was to build it. God told him that He would save Noah and his family when the destruction came.

So Noah started out, and judgment eventually came. God spoke to Noah again and said, "Noah, I'm going to give the world seven more days, and then the flood will come" (see Genesis 7:4).

Today the only bright spot on the horizon of this world is the promise of the coming again of Christ, the Messiah. We can't go on much longer morally. We can't go on much longer scientifically. The technology that was supposed to save us is ready to destroy us. New weapons are being made all the time, including chemical and biological weapons.

In the New Testament we read that Christ told His followers that He would come again. He said that He was leaving so that He could prepare a place for them.

Jesus promised that He is coming back, and we are to comfort one another with His words. We're not to wait in terror, because as believers we have the hope of the coming again of Christ.

Prayer *for the* Day:

Jesus, help me to live each day by faith, knowing that You have prepared a place for me and that You will come again. Thank You that, because of my faith in You, I have confidence that I will be with You for eternity.

Believe in the Lord Jesus, and you will be saved—you and your household. —ACTS 16:31

You *and* Your Family

Noah was the grandson of Methuselah. He was the son of Lamech. There is no mention of faith in the lives of Noah's grandfather or father. They may have been believers, but there is no mention of it in the Bible. I think the record is there to indicate that faith is not passed on automatically from one generation to the next. It requires a choice by each of us in each generation.

Noah started building the ark, and as Noah built the ship, his work was a sermon to the people of that day: "Repent, believe. Let God come into your heart. Let God take control of your life. Come into the ark and be saved." But no one repented. Then one day God said to Noah, "Come into the ark, you and your family."

The Bible says a great deal about entire families coming to

Christ. Rahab the harlot was saved by the grace of God; but her father, mother, brothers, and the entire family were saved in Jericho with her. The Philippian jailer was saved with his entire household. The entire household of Cornelius, the Roman centurion, was saved. That could be true in your family too. You may be the one who could lead your family to Christ. If you take your stand for Christ, they may come to Him too.

Prayer *for the* Day:

Guide me, Jesus, as I take a stand for You, so that my family and others will want a relationship with You too. Through your Holy Spirit, draw my loved ones into a saving knowledge of You.

Cast all your anxiety on him because he cares for you.
—1 PETER 5:7

Alone *but not* Lonely

S ome time ago we received a letter from a radio listener who for five years had been crippled into a sitting position by arthritis. For five painful years she was unable to stretch out or to lie down, yet she wrote, "I have spent many a day alone, but never a lonely day." Why? It was Christ who made the difference. With Christ as your Savior and constant Companion, you, too—although alone—need never be lonely.

In John 11, we read of Mary and Martha. Lazarus, their brother, was dead. Jesus had not yet come. They stood beside his body and wept.

For you, too, perhaps the world has become a vast cemetery containing but one grave. You have stood in the sick room and watched the one dearer than all the world to you slip beyond your reach.

You crave fellowship. You want someone to come along with a helping hand to wipe the tears away, put the smile back on your face, and give you joy through the sorrow. Jesus can do just that.

God loves His children. If you are willing to trust Him and give yourself to Him, He can carry your sorrow.

Prayer *for the* Day:

Heavenly Father, I trust You, and I ask You to carry my sorrow and suffering. Be my ever-present Companion and take away my loneliness today.

There is a friend who sticks closer than a brother.
—Proverbs 18:24

Warmth *of the* Fire

A few years ago a beautiful young Hollywood star, with apparently everything a young woman could want, ended her life. In the brief note that she left was an incredibly simple explanation—she was unbearably lonely.

After the death of her husband, Queen Victoria of England said, "There is no one left to call me Victoria." Even though she was a queen, she knew what it meant to be lonely.

Author H.G. Wells said on his birthday, "I am 65, and I am lonely and have never found peace."

The psalmist said, *"I am forgotten by them as though I were dead; I have become like broken pottery"* (Psalm 31:12).

One kind of loneliness is the loneliness of solitude. The sentry standing duty alone at an outpost, the thousands in mental institutions, and those in solitary confinement in prisons and concentration camps know the loneliness of solitude. Louis Zamperini, the great Olympic track star, told of the loneliness of solitude on a life raft where he spent 47 days during World War II.

The second loneliness is the loneliness of society. That poor person living in the dingy apartment who never receives a letter, who never hears one word of encouragement, who never experiences the handclasp of a friend—that wealthy society leader whose money has bought everything but love and happiness—each knows a loneliness few can understand.

You have a Friend who sticks closer than a brother. Jesus Christ makes life joyful, satisfying, and glorious to you, if you have repented, surrendered, and committed your heart and life to Him. Christ forgives your past sins, and He takes you into His family; He brings you to the hearth, and you feel the warmth of the fire. If you are lonely today, seek Christ and know the fellowship that He brings.

Prayer *for the* Day:

Dear Jesus, be the Friend that I need in my times of loneliness. Help me to reach out in friendship and love to others who may be alone.

Holy, holy, holy is the Lord God Almighty, who was, and is, and is to come. —REVELATION 4:8

Unchanging Character

God is unchanging in His holiness. God is a holy God, a righteous God.

God is unchanging in His judgment. A day is coming in which all of us will stand before the judgment of Almighty God to give an account of our lives; we will give an account of what we did with His Son, Jesus Christ, and of our response to Him when He said, "I love you, I want to forgive you, I want to change you, I want to be your Friend." What will we answer? What will we do with Christ? The Bible says, *"The Lord will judge the ends of the earth"* (1 Samuel 2:10).

God is also unchanging in His love: *"God demonstrates his own love for us in this: While we were still sinners, Christ died for us"* (Romans 5:8). God loves us! God is interested in us.

He has the hairs of our heads numbered. He knows all about us, and He loves us!

God loves us with a love that we do not understand. When we come to Christ and give our hearts and lives to Him, He will give *agape* love—His love—to us so that we can love people whom we usually don't even like. He will give us a supernatural power to love.

Prayer *for the* Day:

Dear God, I am grateful for Your unchanging holiness, righteousness, and love. Thank You for loving me. Give me Your love for the people that You bring into my life.

As for God, his way is perfect; the word of the Lord is flawless.
—2 SAMUEL 22:31

Life *as* It Is

God's laws for the spiritual world are found in the Bible. Whatever else there may be that tells us of God, it is more clearly told in the Bible.

Nature in her laws tells of God, but the message is not too clear. It tells us nothing of the love and grace of God. Conscience, in our inmost being, does tell us of God, but the message is fragmentary.

The only place we can find a clear, unmistakable message is in the Word of God, which we call the Bible. If the Bible is not true, then everything I have been preaching has no foundation.

True Christianity finds all of its doctrines in the Bible; true Christianity does not deny any part of the Bible; true Christianity does not add anything to the Bible. For many centuries the Bible has been the most available book on the earth. It has no hidden purpose. It cannot be destroyed.

The Bible has a magnificent heritage. It has 66 books, written over a period of 1,600 years by more than 30 writers, and yet the message is the same throughout—so clearly so that the 66 books are actually one book.

The message, in every part, is straightforward. No writer changed his message to put his friends in a better light. The sins of small and great alike are frankly admitted, and life is presented as it actually is.

Prayer *for the* Day:

Dear God, I believe that Your Word is true and that it is the foundation for life. As I read and study the Bible each day, reveal to me Your message and show me how to apply it to my life.

For the word of God is living and active. Sharper than any double-edged sword, it penetrates even to dividing soul and spirit, joints and marrow; it judges the thoughts and attitudes of the heart. —HEBREWS 4:12

Purges *and* Bonfires

The Bible will always be the center of controversy. For many centuries there have been purges and bonfires. There are Bibles in existence today that were baked into loaves of bread to keep them from the hands of leaders who wanted to destroy the Word of God.

There are Bibles in scores of languages; and organizations are working around the clock to provide Bible portions for remote tribes so that they, too, may have something of God's Word.

Robert E. Lee once said, "The Bible is a book in comparison with which all others in my eyes are of minor importance, and which in all my perplexities and distresses has never failed to give me light and strength."

You may ask me today, "What is the message of the Bible?" The message of the Bible is Jesus Christ.

The Bible is concerned only incidentally with the history of Israel or with a system of ethics. The Bible is primarily concerned with the story of man's redemption as it is in Jesus Christ. If you read Scripture and miss the story of salvation, you have missed its message and its meaning.

The story of Jesus can be traced through the Bible.

The message of Jesus Christ, our Savior, is the story of the Bible—it is the story of salvation; it is the story of the Gospel; it is the story of life, peace, eternity, and Heaven. The whole world ought to know the story of the Bible.

Prayer *for the* Day:

I know that Your Word, dear Lord, is living and active. Give me boldness to share the message of salvation with those around me, even in the face of opposition.

Without faith it is impossible to please God. —HEBREWS 11:6

The Need *for* Faith

Humans have five physical senses: We can see, hear, taste, smell, and touch. We have a body with eyes, ears, mouth, nose, hands, and feet. But we are more than a body; we are a living soul.

Our soul is that part of our being which possesses intelligence, conscience, and memory— the real personality. Your body will die, but your soul lives on. And that soul has a "sixth sense"—the ability to believe, to have faith.

The Bible teaches that faith is the only approach we have to God. *"Anyone who comes to* [God] *must believe that he exists and that he rewards those who earnestly seek him"* (Hebrews 11:6). Faith pleases God more than anything else.

Cliff Barrows and I have been close friends for years.

Suppose I went to him and said, "Cliff, you are a wonderful person, but I don't believe a thing you say." How would he feel? That is the way some people treat God.

You may be saying, "God, I believe You are great, but I do not believe Your Word; I do not believe what You say." In order to please God you must believe Him. God and God's Word are inseparable.

Prayer *for the* Day:

Dear God, I believe You are great, and I do believe what You say. I want to live in a way that demonstrates that I trust Your Word.

Now faith is being sure of what we hope for and certain of what we do not see. —HEBREWS 11:1

We Must Choose

Faith implies four things: self-renunciation, reliance with utter confidence on Christ, obedience, and a changed life.

To have faith implies self-renunciation. The problems of the world are not from without. They are not political, social, or economic in origin. Christ said that all of these evil things come from within. Our soul has a disease called sin.

What is sin? Sin is transgression, lawbreaking, coming short of God's standards. You break a law of your country and you are a lawbreaker. You break the moral law of God and you are a lawbreaker. Every person who has ever lived is a lawbreaker; he or she is a sinner in God's sight.

Christ did not die by accident. He died voluntarily in our

place. God took all of your sins and laid them on Christ. God says He will not forgive you, He will not transform you, He will not give you the peace and joy that you search for, until you choose between your sins and Christ. The moment you turn from your sins and turn to Christ, you are forgiven.

He can break the chain of every sin that binds you if you are willing to give it up. The moment you receive Christ by faith, He comes into your heart and gives you power to overcome sin.

Second, faith implies reliance with utter confidence in Christ. Although we cannot see Him, hear Him, or touch Him, we can believe in Christ and rely upon Him.

Third, faith implies obedience; and obedience implies action. We must be faithful to put the teachings of Christ into practice in our daily lives.

Prayer *for the* Day:

Heavenly Father, forgive me for the times when I fall short of Your standards. Show me how I can obey You more fully and more faithfully each day.

So keep up your courage, men, for I have faith in God that it will happen just as he told me. —ACTS 27:25

Finding *a* Song *to* Sing

Sir Winston Churchill once made the statement, "Our problems are beyond us." Dr. Nathan Pusey, president of Harvard University from 1953 to 1971, said that the whole world is searching for a creed to believe and a song to sing.

Where are we going to turn? The Apostle Paul, many years ago, faced that question from the crew of his storm-tossed ship. He said, "*Men, you should have taken my advice not to sail from Crete; then you would have spared yourselves this damage and loss. But now I urge you to keep up your courage, because not one of you will be lost; only the ship will be destroyed. Last night an angel of the God whose I am and whom I serve stood beside me and said, 'Do not be afraid, Paul'*" (Acts 27:21–24).

The angry waves lashed against the ship, the lightning

flashed, the thunder roared, yet Paul stood in the midst of the storm and declared, "I have faith in God."

There are storms in the world today: storms of unbelief, materialism, secularism, moral degeneracy, and international difficulties.

And there are storms in your own life: storms of temptation, confusion, and difficulty. Perhaps by neglecting church, by neglecting daily Bible reading and prayer, you have broken away from moral moorings and you are out in a storm.

You thought that you could find some satisfaction, pleasure, or peace; but you have not found it. An uneasy conscience says, "Stop before it is too late!"

Some people think that going to church on Sunday and owning a dust-covered Bible makes a person a Christian. That is not true. A Christian is one in whom Christ dwells, and the person's life will give evidence of this. The moment you receive Christ by faith, He comes into your heart and life. He gives you a love for what is good and the power to do it. He gives you a new song to sing.

Prayer *for the* Day:

Despite the storms in my life, Jesus, You have given me a new song. Hold me fast to Your side when the waves threaten to overwhelm me.

Day 13

If you have faith as small as a mustard seed, you can say to this mountain, "Move from here to there" and it will move. Nothing will be impossible for you. —MATTHEW 17:20

Just *a* Little Thread

The suspension bridge at Niagara Falls was started by a thread attached to a kite. When the wind was favorable, the kite went across. Then on the thread they put a string and pulled it across.

Faith implies conversion, or a change in one's life. Jesus said to Matthew, "Follow Me," and Matthew immediately got up and followed Him. Jesus said to the rich young ruler, "Follow Me," and the young ruler went away sorrowful.

Matthew chose to follow Christ.

The rich young ruler rejected Christ and went his way.

Every one of us is faced with this choice.

Your faith may be just a little thread. It may be small and weak, but act on that faith. It does not matter how big your faith is, but rather, where your faith is. Is it in Christ, the Son of God, who died on the cross for your sins?

Let Christ bring peace and joy to your soul. Let Him change your life of defeat and confusion into one of purpose and peace.

Prayer *for the* Day:

As I place my faith in You, Lord Jesus, change my defeat and confusion into purpose and peace. Increase my faith today.

Do not conform any longer to the pattern of this world, but be transformed by the renewing of your mind. Then you will be able to test and approve what God's will is—his good, pleasing and perfect will. —ROMANS 12:2

No Compromise

When Rome was at the height of her glory and power, there appeared a disturbing sect called Christians. Because of a fire that burned within them, these people dared to be different.

In an era when immorality, lavishness, and luxury were stylish, they refused to be defiled by the sensual practices of a disintegrating civilization. In a period when human life was cheap they put a high value upon human beings, their souls, and their destiny.

These Christians refused to be absorbed into the godless society of Rome. They had not heard of the rule that we hear today, "When in Rome, do as the Romans do." The Roman high tribunal then initiated a drive to stamp out Christianity as a disturber of pagan unity.

The Romans had a false notion that a person's conscience could be controlled by law, so they made it illegal to be different. All must bow to Caesar. All must conform to pagan custom. All must behave like true Romans. Nonconformists were threatened with death, and many chose death rather than conform to Rome and compromise their consciences.

Times have changed, but human nature hasn't. Though the methods are different, the pagan world is still trying to put its stamp of conformity on every follower of Jesus Christ. Every possible pressure is being brought to bear upon Christians to make them conform to the standards of the present world.

I'm asking you to be a committed follower of Jesus Christ, not conformed to the world, but being daily conformed to the image of the person of Jesus Christ.

Prayer *for the* Day:

In spite of the pressures to conform to the world, God, make me into a reflection of You. Conform me into the image of Christ, and give me the strength to live without compromise.

If the world hates you, keep in mind that it hated me first.
—JOHN 15:18

Afraid *to be* Different

I n our desire to make Christ known and to increase the influence of the church, we are many times prone to think that Christians and the church can be made popular with the unbelieving world.

This is a grave mistake on the part of the church. Christ crucified is anathema to Satan, and the message of the Gospel is still a stumbling block and foolishness to the world. The Apostle John writes, *"Do not be surprised, my brothers, if the world hates you"* (1 John 3:13).

When the Christian or the church becomes popular with the unbelieving world, something is seriously wrong with the Christian or the church. Because Christ runs counter to evil and because we are Christ-owned, we must also stand against evil.

Christians may be shown a grudging respect at times, but

if we are faithful to Him, we will surely incur the wrath of the world. *"In fact, everyone who wants to live a godly life in Christ Jesus will be persecuted,"* says the Scripture (2 Timothy 3:12).

The Scripture teaches that popularity with the world means death. Satan's most effective tool is conformity and compromise. He is aware that one man standing in the midst of a pagan people can move more people in the direction of God than thousands of insipid professors of religion when he declares, *"I am not ashamed of the gospel of Christ: for it is the power of God unto salvation"* (Romans 1:16, KJV).

Prayer *for the* Day:

Lord Jesus, remind me daily that the world hated You first, and give me courage to declare Your Gospel even though others may hate me. Help me to remember that the power of the Gospel results in salvation.

I want to remind you of the gospel I preached to you, which you received and on which you have taken your stand. By this gospel you are saved, if you hold firmly to the word I preached to you.
—1 CORINTHIANS 15:1—2

Daring *to* Believe

The Apostle Paul urges Christians everywhere in all ages to be nonconformists as far as the world system is concerned. We are not to conform. A true Christian, living an obedient life, is a constant rebuke to those who accept the moral standards of this world.

Patrick Henry, with his heroic declaration, "Give me liberty or give me death," did more for the cause of freedom than a million who were bent on saving their own skins.

Martin Luther, standing before the Diet of Worms, saying, "Here I stand, so help me God, I can do no other," did more to further the cause of religious liberty than a million conformists who had lost the vitality of true religion.

We often ask ourselves, "How could the early disciples turn the world upside down when millions of Christians can't even keep it right side up today?"

The answer is a simple one. They didn't conform their faith to match the world. They had the truth, and they refused to water it down. They held a faith that would not compromise.

Because they dared to buck the tide of public opinion and be different; because they dared to believe when other people doubted; because they were willing to risk their lives for what they stood for; because they chose death rather than to live an empty life, the world took notice of what motivated these men and women. In due time the philosophical and religious world was turned upside down.

Prayer *for the* Day:

Through the power of the Holy Spirit, dear Lord, let me be able to stand for what is right and true in the face of unbelief and opposition. Show me how to hold firmly to Your Word.

The mystery of godliness is great. —1 TIMOTHY 3:16

Looking *at the* Underside

My grandmother used to make quilts. As a little boy, I couldn't figure out by looking at the underside what the quilt would look like without looking on the top side to see the pattern that she was making.

Sometimes when I board an airplane there are dark clouds and it is raining. But in a few minutes the plane is above the clouds and the sun is shining. I can assure you that above the clouds in your life the sun is shining. God is still there despite any tragedy that you may be experiencing.

Why does God allow tragedy? In 1976 we were in Guatemala when a terrible earthquake occurred, and it seemed that almost the whole country was sinking. The president asked me if I would go on television to explain to the people why God would allow such a tragedy to happen to their country.

On November 21, 1980, when the MGM Grand Hotel in Las Vegas burned, survivors were brought into the Convention Center, where our Crusade meetings were being held. In an interview Governor Robert List talked about the good times at the MGM only 24 hours before. "And how quickly," he said, "the music has stopped."

When I was asked to explain these tragedies, I had to say, "There's a mystery to tragedies like this. We don't know the answer." And we may never know until God explains all things to us.

Only He can see the other side of our lives. We may not understand, but we have a God who loves us and is *an ever-present help in trouble*" (Psalm 46:1).

Prayer *for the* Day:

Heavenly Father, I know that You see the pattern You are making in my life. Help me to not allow the trials to block my vision of You.

The King will reply, "I tell you the truth, whatever you did for one of the least of these brothers of mine, you did for me."
—MATTHEW 25:40

The Mystery *of* Life

For humans, there is a mystery as to why God created the earth. There is a mystery as to why He put people on this earth. But God has revealed answers through the Bible and through the person of His Son, Jesus Christ. In the Bible you will find the answers to the questions and the problems of your life.

But man rebelled against God. Man said, "I don't need You, God. I can build my world without You." God said, "If you take that position, you will suffer and die." Man took that position, and he began to suffer, and he has been dying ever since. Physical death is just the death of the body, but the spirit lives on. If your spirit is separated from God for eternity, it will be lost forever.

The Bible teaches that Satan is the author of sin. Sin is the reason that we have afflictions, including death. All of our problems and our suffering, including death itself, are a result of man's rebellion against God. But God has provided a rescue in the person of His Son, Jesus Christ. That's why Christ died on the cross. That's why He rose from the dead.

In suffering there is a message of compassion. Jesus said, *"For I was hungry and you gave me something to eat, I was thirsty and you gave me something to drink, I was a stranger and you invited me in, I needed clothes and you clothed me, I was sick and you looked after me, I was in prison and you came to visit me"* (Matthew 25:35–36). As fire swept through the MGM Grand Hotel in 1980, I saw the emergency crews, the military people, The Salvation Army, the Red Cross, the doctors, the nurses, and the people coming to donate clothes and food. I saw compassion in action.

Prayer *for the* Day:

I may not understand why suffering comes, but I can show compassion to those who suffer. Lord, help me to be Your hands and feet to others in need.

Day 19

[God] comforts us in all our tribulations, that we may be able to comfort those who are in any trouble. —2 CORINTHIANS 1:4, NKJV

One *in* Christ

In suffering there is a message of unity. Isaac's twin sons, Jacob and Esau, had been feuding and fighting. But when Isaac died, they came to bury him. Because of their father's death, the two sons came together. (See Genesis 35:29.)

Jesus prayed *"that all of them may be one, Father, just as you are in me and I am in you"* (John 17:21). And that's the way we ought to be as Christians: one in Christ. If you have been born into the family of God, you are a child of God. You are brothers and sisters.

Suffering holds a message of comfort. In 2 Corinthians we read, *"Praise be to the God and Father of our Lord Jesus Christ, the Father of compassion and the God of all comfort, who comforts us in all our troubles, so that we can comfort those in* any trouble with the comfort we ourselves have received from God" (2 Corinthians 1:3–4).

Because tragedy happened to you, it gives you a greater sense of oneness with others who experience tragedy. You can feel for them in that suffering situation. Because we have been comforted through the Word of God, we in turn may be able to comfort others.

Prayer *for the* Day:

Dear God, use the trials in my life to unite me with my brothers and sisters in Christ. Enable me to share Your comfort with others who are suffering.

Day 20

If we are distressed, it is for your comfort and salvation; if we are comforted, it is for your comfort, which produces in you patient endurance of the same sufferings we suffer. — 2 CORINTHIANS 1:6

Telescopes *to* Heaven

What should be our attitude toward suffering? First, it should be one of worship. We ought to say, "O God, I believe You are the great and mighty God. I don't understand all the things that are happening in my life, but, O God, I trust in You."

Second, we should ask God to teach us all He would have us learn about Him, about ourselves, about others and how we can minister to those who are suffering.

Third, our attitude in suffering should glorify God. People are going to watch us as Christians. They will ask, "How is it that Christ is so in control of his or her life that he or she was able to help others?"

Jesus suffered and died for us on the cross, but God raised Him from the dead. Jesus Christ now sits at the right hand

39

of God the Father, and He sees our suffering. He sees our life every day and knows exactly where we stand.

The Bible teaches that we are to be patient in suffering. That's the hardest thing of all, to be patient, to have songs in the night. Tears become telescopes to Heaven, bringing eternity a little closer.

Prayer *for the* Day:

Thank You, Jesus, because You endured the cross and You know what I am going through today. Give me patience and an attitude that glorifies You in spite of my pain.

Day 21

Everyone who calls on the name of the Lord will be saved.
—ROMANS 10:13

Like Stray Sheep

Jesus was *"despised and rejected by men, a man of sorrows, and familiar with suffering. Like one from whom men hide their faces he was despised, and we esteemed him not. Surely he took up our infirmities and carried our sorrows, yet we considered him stricken by God, smitten by him, and afflicted. But he was pierced for our transgressions, he was crushed for our iniquities; the punishment that brought us peace was upon him, and by his wounds we are healed. We all, like sheep, have gone astray, each of us has turned to his own way; and the Lord has laid on him the iniquity of us all"* (Isaiah 53:3–6).

Jesus was alone. He had come to His own, and His own did not receive Him. When He was being arrested in the Garden of Gethsemane, we are told that *"all the disciples deserted him and fled"* (Matthew 26:56).

The crowds who had so recently shouted "hosanna" would soon shout, "Crucify Him! Crucify Him!" (see Matthew 21:9; 27:22–23). Now even His loyal twelve had left.

And at last we hear Him cry out, *My God, my God, why have you forsaken me?* (Mark 15:34). Not only had He been forsaken by His human companions, but now in that desperate and lonely hour, He—because He was bearing our sins in His own body on the cross—had been forsaken by God. Jesus was enduring the suffering and judgment of Hell for you and for me.

Hell, essentially, is separation from God. Hell is the loneliest place in the universe. Jesus suffered its agony for you, in your place. Now God says, "Repent, believe on Christ, receive Christ, and you will never know the sorrow, the loneliness, and the agony of Hell."

If you have not already received Christ as Savior, will you call on Him today?

Prayer *for the* Day:

Dear Lord Jesus, I know that I am a sinner, and I ask for Your forgiveness. I believe You died for my sins and rose from the dead. I turn from my sins and invite You to come into my life. I want to trust and follow You as my Lord and Savior.

Precious in the sight of the Lord is the death of his saints.
—PSALM 116:15

No Accidents

Some of you have been stunned by the sudden passing of a consecrated person, a godly pastor, a devout missionary, or a saintly mother. You have stood at the open grave with hot tears coursing down your cheeks and have asked in utter bewilderment, "Why, O God, why?"

Allow me to assure you that the death of the righteous is no accident. Do you think that the God whose watchful vigil notes the sparrow's fall and who knows the number of hairs on our heads would turn His back on one of His children in the hour of peril? With Him there are no accidents, no tragedies, and no catastrophes as far as His children are concerned.

Paul, who lived most of his Christian life on the brink of death, expressed triumphant certainty about life beyond this realm of time and space. His rugged, disciplined soul took trouble, persecution, injustice, pain, thwarted plans, and broken dreams in stride.

He never bristled in questioning cynicism and asked, "Why, Lord?" He knew beyond the shadow of a doubt that his life was being fashioned into the image and likeness of his blessed Redeemer; and despite the discomfort, he never flinched in the process.

Paul believed in Christ and committed his all to Christ. The result was that he knew Christ was able to keep him against that day. Strong faith is the result of unconditional commitment to Jesus Christ.

Prayer *for the* Day:

Heavenly Father, thank You for Your reassurance that there is hope beyond the grave and that You watch over every one of Your children. Continue to fashion me into the image and likeness of Your Son.

Then I heard a voice from heaven say, "Write: Blessed are the dead who die in the Lord from now on." —REVELATION 14:13

A Rest *from* Labor

One of the bonuses of being a Christian is the wonderful hope that extends out beyond the grave into the glory of God's tomorrow. The Bible opens with a tragedy and ends in a triumph. In Genesis we see the devastation of sin and death, but in Revelation we see victory over sin and death.

The death of the righteous is distinctively different. It is not to be feared—it is not to be shunned. It is the shadowed threshold to the palace of God. No wonder Balaam said, *"Let me die the death of the righteous, and may my end be like theirs!"* (Numbers 23:10).

There is a vast difference between the death of sinner and saint. I have talked to doctors and nurses who have held the hands of dying people, and they say that there is as much difference between the death of a Christian and of a non-Christian as there is between Heaven and Hell.

The Bible speaks of death, for a Christian, as a rest from labor. The Bible says, *"They will rest from their labor, for their deeds will follow them"* (Revelation 14:13). It is as if the Lord of the harvest says to the weary laborer, "You have been faithful in your task; come and sit in the sheltered porch of my palace and rest from your labors—enter now into the joy of your Lord."

Some of God's saints accomplish more in a few years than others do in a lifetime. The Bible says, *"There remains, then, a Sabbath-rest for the people of God"* (Hebrews 4:9). That rest cannot begin until the angel of death takes them by the hand and leads them into the glorious presence of their Lord.

Prayer *for the* Day:

As You promised, God, I look forward to the day when You will give me rest. While I wait, give me the strength to accomplish the tasks that You have set before me.

Day 24

We are confident, I say, and would prefer to be away from the body and at home with the Lord. —2 CORINTHIANS 5:8

Pulling *up* Anchor

The Bible speaks of death as a departure. When Paul approached the valley of the shadow of death he did not shudder with fear; rather he announced with a note of triumph, *"The time has come for my departure"* (2 Timothy 4:6).

The word *departure* literally means "to pull up anchor and to set sail." Everything that happens prior to death is a preparation for the journey. Death marks the beginning, not the end. It is a solemn, dramatic step in our journey to God.

Many times I said farewell to my wife as I departed for Europe or some other distant destination. Separation always brings a tinge of sadness, but there is the high hope that we shall meet again. In the meantime, the flame of love burned brightly in her heart and in mine.

The Bible says we are pilgrims and strangers in a foreign land. This world is not our home; our citizenship is in Heaven.

This is like the hope of the believing Christian who stands at the grave of a loved one who is with the Lord. The Christian says "goodbye," but only until the day breaks and the shadows flee away.

Prayer *for the* Day:

Lord, it is never easy to say goodbye. Give me grace to approach the time of departure as Paul did, remembering that death for a Christian is only a temporary separation from loved ones but the beginning of an eternity with You.

To them God has chosen to make known among the Gentiles the glorious riches of this mystery, which is Christ in you, the hope of glory. —COLOSSIANS 1:27

From Attic *to* Cellar

The resurrected Christ lives today, but in another very real sense: in the heart of every true believer. Though Jesus is in His glorified body in Heaven, yet through the Holy Spirit He dwells in the heart of every Christian. The Christ of God, in whom *"all the fullness of the Deity lives in bodily form"* (Colossians 2:9), lives within the hearts of people. This is a mystery that is beyond comprehension and yet is gloriously true.

When we come to Jesus Christ, we bring everything that we have. Our bodies with all their members, our faculties, our talents, our time, our money, our possessions, our hearts, our will, are all His. Our faces become the faces in which the resurrected Christ shows forth His beauty and His glory. Our eyes become the eyes of the resurrected Christ, to exhibit His sympathy and His tenderness. Our lips become the lips of the resurrected Christ, to speak His messages. Our ears become the ears of the resurrected Christ, sensitive to every cry of spiritual need. Our minds become the mind of the resurrected Christ, instruments for the realization of His purpose. Our hands become the hands of the resurrected Christ, to act on His impulse and allow Him to work through us. Our feet tread the narrow path that the Savior trod, keeping in step with Him throughout the earthly pilgrimage.

Allow the resurrected Christ to allocate your time as His own; to control your money as His own; to energize your talents, your zeal, and your ability with His resurrected life; to have complete right-of-way throughout your being. He does not want an apartment in your house. He claims your entire home from attic to cellar.

Prayer *for the* Day:

Lord, help me to demonstrate my faith in You by allowing You to take full control of my life. I want to see with Your eyes, to think with Your mind, and to allow You to work through me in everything that I do.

The ground of a certain rich man produced a good crop. He thought to himself ... "You have plenty of good things laid up for many years. Take life easy." ... But God said to him, "You fool! This very night your life will be demanded from you." —LUKE 12:16–20

Whose Plans?

Some people imagine that to possess wealth is a good thing. When they hear of someone winning a rich prize, they admit that they would gladly be in his place. They think of security as being a relief from financial strain that only wealth can bring. They dream of the many things that they could purchase.

The rich man in this story felt secure. He thought he did not need God, he did not need prayer, for he had so much else. He hardened his heart, stifled his conscience, and dulled his mind. He did not think of the possibility of death and the judgment of God. He felt that his financial security was a bulwark against all evil.

We may say to ourselves, "I will plan carefully. I will do this or do that." But God can say, "I have other plans for you."

We may try to be masters of our own circumstances and lord of our own destinies. We may try to maneuver people and situations to suit our ends and get our own way. Our plans may succeed for a time, as they seemed to succeed for a time for the rich man in the story Jesus told, but what folly and tragedy it proved to be! This road leads to destruction.

It is not only money, bank accounts, investments, and insurance policies that Christ is talking about. If a man is rich in anything apart from God—whether it be talents, brains, abilities, or popularity—he is in no less danger than this rich man.

Prayer *for the* Day:

Forgive me when I make plans that exclude You, Lord God. Keep me from having a hardened heart. Instead, fill my heart with You.

It is easier for a camel to go through the eye of a needle than for a rich man to enter the kingdom of God. —MATTHEW 19:24

Luxury *and* Riches

Fifteen hundred years ago the people of imperial Rome were living in luxury, ease, and prosperity. The Romans laughed at the rugged barbarians of the north. They had a far lower standard of living than the Romans did. They could not possibly conquer Rome—great imperial Rome. Yet they did. Those illiterate barbarians conquered rich and luxurious Rome, because Rome had become morally and spiritually weak. The city fell almost without a fight.

Jesus spoke of the deceitfulness of riches and prosperity. When we possess riches, we may be deceived about our positions in life. We may tend to feel independent, to rely on and to trust in our own riches rather than in God. We may start to feel safe apart from God and forget that we may die at any moment.

There is nothing in the teachings of Jesus to indicate that it is wrong to be rich. Jesus talked about the motives, thoughts, and intents of the heart. He spoke about covetousness and stewardship.

God requires that we should have riches toward Him. He demands an inward righteousness which the world cannot always see—but which is always before God. God looks for riches in the heart and the soul.

To the rich young ruler, Jesus said, *"If you want to be perfect, go, sell your possessions and give to the poor, and you will have treasure in heaven. Then come, follow me"* (Matthew 19:21).

Our world will someday fall apart. The Bible teaches that our buildings will crumble and fall and everything in this world will pass away, *"but he who does the will of God abides forever"* (1 John 2:17, NKJV). Christ is the only security we have.

Prayer *for the* Day:

Dear Jesus, if I have riches of this world, show me how I can use them to further Your kingdom. When I am in want, keep me from coveting what others have. In every situation, help me to trust in You for my security.

I urge you, brothers, in view of God's mercy, to offer your bodies as living sacrifices, holy and pleasing to God—this is your spiritual act of worship. —ROMANS 12:1

Like *the* Gulf Stream

These bodies of ours are intended to be temples of the Spirit of God. We are not to prostrate them before the temples of Baal. We are to present them wholly to God as a "living sacrifice." Our dress, our posture, our actions should all be for the honor and glory of Christ.

Much of our talk as Christians is secular, not spiritual. It is easy to fall into the conversational conformity of the world and spend an evening discussing politics, new cars, and the latest entertainment. We often forget that we are to edify one another with holy conversation, and that our conversation should be on heavenly, and not exclusively on earthly, things.

God's purpose for us is that we ought to be conformed to the image of His Son. The world may exert its pressure to deform us, but we are told, "*Be transformed by the renewing of your mind"* (Romans 12:2).

The world attempts to absorb us into its secular society and to conform us to its earthly image, but Christ urges us not to conform. Clearly He says of those who believe in Him, *"They are not of the world, even as I am not of it"* (John 17:16).

The Gulf Stream is in the ocean, and yet it is not a part of it. Believers are in the world, and yet they must not be absorbed by it. The Gulf Stream maintains its warm temperatures even in the icy water of the North Atlantic. If Christians are to fulfill their purposes in the world, they must not be chilled by the indifferent, godless society in which they live.

Prayer *for the* Day:

Lord, help me to keep my body and my words pure and holy, acceptable to You. Make my life a pleasing sacrifice that glorifies You.

Day 29

Your attitude should be the same as that of Christ Jesus.
—Philippians 2:5

Call *to* Battle

The words of the Apostle Paul, "Be not conformed to this world," have tremendous significance and meaning for us today. These words cut like a sharp sword across our way of life. They are not comfortable words. They have the tone of the battle call in them. They separate the weak from the strong. But they are words of inspiration, and we need to hear them today.

Be not conformed to this world mentally. The world by its advertisements, its conversation, and its philosophy is engaged in a gigantic brainwashing task. Not always consciously but sometimes unconsciously, the Christian is beset by secular and worldly propaganda.

Much entertainment is slanted to those who feed on violence, sex, and lawlessness. It seems that some diabolic mastermind is running the affairs of this world and that his chief objective is to brainwash Christians and to get them to conform to this world.

The world's sewage system threatens to contaminate the stream of Christian thought. Satan will contest every hour you spend in Bible reading or prayer.

However, above the din we can hear the voice of Scripture, *"Be transformed by the renewing of your mind. Then you will be able to test and approve what God's will is—his good, pleasing and perfect will"* (Romans 12:2).

We Christians are not even to be conformed to the world's anxieties. Many Christians are wringing their hands and saying, "What's the world coming to?"

The Bible has already told us that "the world and the lust thereof" are going to pass away. We have already been told in Scripture that the world is coming to a cataclysmic judgment.

We Christians are to be lights in the midst of darkness, and our lives should exemplify relaxation, peace, and joy in the midst of frustration, confusion, and despair.

Prayer *for the* Day:

Dear Jesus, in a world of confusion and despair, reflect Your light through my life. Prepare me for trials that may lie ahead by giving me Your peace and joy.

The evil deeds of a wicked man ensnare him; the cords of his sin hold him fast. —PROVERBS 5:22

Cords *of* Sin

Think of it, cords of sin hold you in some of your habits that you know to be wrong and sinful. It may be a drug habit; it may be an alcohol habit; it may be a sex habit; it may be something else. Too many people think that they can go out and sow their wild oats all week and then head for the church on Sunday and everything is OK.

Everything is not OK. You may have been baptized and confirmed and you may go to church. But Sunday is one day, and the rest of the week is something else—in your business life, in your home life.

It is not just becoming a Christian; it is also being a Christian all the time, 24 hours a day. It is bearing the fruit of the Spirit, which the Holy Spirit supernaturally produces in you when you come to know Christ.

The Bible talks about *"all that is in the world"* as being *"the lust of the flesh, the lust of the eyes, and the pride of life"* (1 John 2:16, NKJV). A meaning of the word *lust* is "selfish desire."

It may be in the physical realm, which is *"the lust of the flesh."* It could be the wrong use of sex. It could be gluttony, overdrinking, or overeating. It could be self-indulgences of various sorts.

It may be in the realm of ambition, the vainglory of life. In other words, wanting that job, that position, so badly that you would sell your soul for it. Or that honor, that award. It is wanting something so badly you will do anything to get it. That is one of the tricks of the devil. It is too high a price to pay.

Prayer *for the* Day:

Dear Lord, when I look for satisfaction in the things of the world, show me the dangers that await me there. Send Your Holy Spirit to break the cords of sin in my life and enable me to honor You with my life.

If anyone would come after me, he must deny himself and take up his cross daily and follow me. —LUKE 9:23

No Regrets

There is a high price of commitment. Jesus must become first in your life as your Lord and your Master and your Savior. Jesus never offered a bargain.

What does this verse mean? It may cost you when you come to Christ—it may cost a great deal. For some of you, it will cost you some of your friends. They won't want a person around them who lives a clean life and talks about God and reads the Bible and prays. It becomes embarrassing to them.

It may mean misunderstanding. Jesus told us that His coming divides families. Some will say "yes" and some "no."

C.T. Studd, the famous English cricketer and member of the English XI cricket team, gave away his vast wealth and became a missionary a century ago. His slogan was, "If Jesus Christ be

God, and died for me, then no sacrifice can be too great for me to make for Him." He lost himself for Christ.

In 1912 William Borden, a graduate of Yale University, left one of America's greatest family fortunes to be a missionary to China. He got as far as Egypt and died of cerebral meningitis. He died—and he was only in his 20s—but there was "no reserve, no retreat, no regrets" in his consecration to God.

Then there was Jim Elliot, a generation ago, who became a missionary to Ecuador in South America. He was killed, along with four others. Before he died, he had written this: "He is no fool who gives what he cannot keep to gain what he cannot lose."

Prayer *for the* Day:

Lord Jesus, following You may come with a high price, but it is always worth it. Create in me the desire to serve You no matter the cost.

Sources

"No Shortcuts to Heaven," *Decision* magazine, January 2005: Cords of Sin, No Regrets.

"Nonconformity to the World," *Decision* magazine, February 2005: No Compromise, Afraid to be Different, Daring to Believe, Like the Gulf Stream, Call to Battle.

"The Greatest News Ever Heard," *Decision* magazine, March 2005: From Cellar to Attic.

"Hope in Death," *Decision* magazine, October 2005: No Accidents, A Rest from Labor, Pulling up Anchor.

"Do You Want to Be Wealthy?" *Decision* magazine, January 2006: Whose Plans? Luxury and Riches.

"The Answer to Loneliness," *Decision* magazine, February 2006: Warmth of the Fire, Alone but not Lonely, Like Stray Sheep.

"The Door Is Still Open," *Decision* magazine, March 2006: A Warning and a Promise, You and Your Family.

"Peace vs. Chaos," *Decision* magazine, September 2006: The Rainbow of Hope.

"Suffering: Why Does God Allow It?" *Decision* magazine, June 2007: Looking at the Underside, The Mystery of Life, One in Christ, Telescopes to Heaven.

"Certainty in an Uncertain World," *Decision* magazine, July–August 2007: Unchanging Character.

"Our Bible," *Decision* magazine, July–August 2007: Life as It Is, Purges and Bonfires.

"An Anchor in Your Storm," *Decision* magazine, September 2008: The Need for Faith, We Must Choose, Finding a Song to Sing, Just a Little Thread.

"The Second Coming of Christ," *Decision* magazine, January 2009: A Place Prepared.

Steps to Peace with God

STEP 1 God's Purpose: Peace and Life

God loves you and wants you to experience peace and life—abundant and eternal.

THE BIBLE SAYS ...

"We have peace with God through our Lord Jesus Christ."
Romans 5:1

"For God so loved the world that He gave His only begotten Son, that whoever believes in Him should not perish but have everlasting life."
John 3:16, NKJV

Since God planned for us to have peace and the abundant life right now, why are most people not having this experience?

"I have come that they may have life, and that they may have it more abundantly." *John 10:10, NKJV*

STEP 2 Our Problem: Separation from God

God created us in His own image to have an abundant life. He did not make us as robots to automatically love and obey Him, but gave us a will and a freedom of choice.

We chose to disobey God and go our own willful way. We still make this choice today. This results in separation from God.

THE BIBLE SAYS ...

"For all have sinned and fall short of the glory of God."
Romans 3:23

"For the wages of sin is death, but the gift of God is eternal life in Christ Jesus our Lord." *Romans 6:23*

Our choice results in separation from God.

Our Attempts

Through the ages, individuals have tried in many ways to bridge this gap ... without success ...

THE BIBLE SAYS ...

"There is a way that seems right to a man, but in the end it leads to death." *Proverbs 14:12*

"But your iniquities have separated you from your God; and your sins have hidden His face from you, so that He will not hear." *Isaiah 59:2, NKJV*

There is only one remedy for this problem of separation.

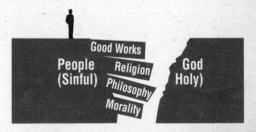

STEP 3 God's Remedy: The Cross

Jesus Christ is the only answer to this problem. He died on the cross and rose from the grave, paying the penalty for our sin and bridging the gap between God and people.

THE BIBLE SAYS ...

"For there is one God and one mediator between God and men, the man Christ Jesus." *1 Timothy 2:5*

"For Christ also suffered once for sins, the just for the unjust, that He might bring us to God." *1 Peter 3:18, NKJV*

"But God demonstrates His own love toward us, in that while we were still sinners, Christ died for us." *Romans 5:8, NKJV*

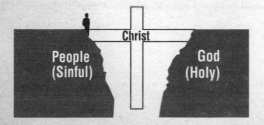

God has provided the only way ... we must make the choice ...

STEP 4   Our Response: Receive Christ

We must trust Jesus Christ and receive Him by personal invitation ...

THE BIBLE SAYS ...

"Behold, I stand at the door and knock. If anyone hears My voice and opens the door, I will come in to him and dine with him, and he with Me." *Revelation 3:20, NKJV*

"But as many as received Him, to them He gave the right to become children of God, to those who believe in His name." *John 1:12, NKJV*

"If you confess with your mouth the Lord Jesus and believe in your heart that God has raised Him from the dead, you will be saved." *Romans 10:9, NKJV*

Are you here ...   *or here?*

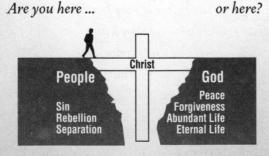

Is there any good reason why you cannot receive Jesus Christ right now?

How to receive Christ:

1. Admit your need (I am a sinner).
2. Be willing to turn from your sins (repent) and ask for God's forgiveness.
3. Believe that Jesus Christ died for you on the cross and rose from the grave.
4. Through prayer, invite Jesus Christ to come in and control your life through the Holy Spirit (receive Jesus as Lord and Savior).

What to Pray:

Dear Lord Jesus,

I know that I am a sinner, and I ask for Your forgiveness. I believe You died for my sins and rose from the dead. I turn from my sins and invite You to come into my heart and life. I want to trust and follow You as my Lord and Savior.

In Your Name, Amen.

_____ _____
Date   Signature

God's Assurance: His Word

If you prayed this prayer,

THE BIBLE SAYS …

"For 'Everyone who calls on the name of the Lord will be saved.'" *Romans 10:13*

Did you sincerely ask Jesus Christ to come into your life? Where is He right now? What has He given you?

"For it is by grace you have been saved, through faith—and this not from yourselves, it is the gift of God—not by works, so that no one can boast." *Ephesians 2:8–9*

The Bible Says ...

"He who has the Son has life; he who does not have the Son of God does not have life. These things I have written to you who believe in the name of the Son of God, that you may know that you have eternal life, and that you may continue to believe in the name of the Son of God." *1 John 5:12–13, NKJV*

Receiving Christ, we are born into God's family through the supernatural work of the Holy Spirit who indwells every believer. This is called regeneration or the "new birth."

This is just the beginning of a wonderful new life in Christ. To deepen this relationship, you should:

1. Read your Bible every day to know Christ better.
2. Talk to God in prayer every day.
3. Tell others about Christ.
4. Worship, fellowship, and serve with other Christians in a church where Christ is preached.
5. As Christ's representative in a needy world, demonstrate your new life by your love and concern for others.

God bless you as you do.
Billy Graham

If you are committing your life to Christ, please let us know! We would like to send you Bible study materials to help you grow in your faith.

The Billy Graham Evangelistic Association exists to support and extend the evangelistic calling and ministries of Billy Graham and Franklin Graham by proclaiming the Gospel of the Lord Jesus Christ to all we can by every effective means available to us and by equipping others to do the same.

Our desire is to introduce as many people as we can to the person of Jesus Christ, so that they might experience His love and forgiveness. Your prayers are the most important way to support us in this ministry. We are grateful for the dedicated prayer support we receive. We are also grateful for those who support us with financial contributions.

Billy Graham Evangelistic Association
1 Billy Graham Parkway
Charlotte, North Carolina 28201-0001
billygraham.org
Toll-free: 1-877-2GRAHAM
(1-877-247-2426)

Billy Graham Evangelistic Association of Canada
20 Hopewell Way NE
Calgary, Alberta T3J 5H5
billygraham.ca
Toll-free: 1-888-393-0003